LANDFORM ADVENTURERS

CANYON HUNTERS

Anita Ganeri

Raintree

www.raintreepublishers.co.uk
Visit our website to find out more information about Raintree books.

To order:
☎ Phone 0845 6044371
📠 Fax +44 (0) 1865 312263
✉ Email myorders@raintreepublishers.co.uk

Customers from outside the UK please telephone +44 1865 312262

Raintree is an imprint of Capstone Global Library Limited, a company incorporated in England and Wales having its registered office at 7 Pilgrim Street, London, EC4V 6LB – Registered company number: 6695582

Text © Capstone Global Library Limited 2012
First published in hardback in 2012
Paperback edition first published in 2013
The moral rights of the proprietor have been asserted.

All rights reserved. No part of this publication may be reproduced in any form or by any means (including photocopying or storing it in any medium by electronic means and whether or not transiently or incidentally to some other use of this publication) without the written permission of the copyright owner, except in accordance with the provisions of the Copyright, Designs and Patents Act 1988 or under the terms of a licence issued by the Copyright Licensing Agency, Saffron House, 6–10 Kirby Street, London EC1N 8TS (www.cla.co.uk). Applications for the copyright owner's written permission should be addressed to the publisher.

Edited by Rebecca Rissman, Dan Nunn, and Sian Smith
Designed by Joanna Hinton Malivoire
Picture research by Elizabeth Alexander
Production by Victoria Fitzgerald
Originated by Capstone Global Library
Printed and bound in China by CTPS

ISBN 978 1 406 22568 6 (hardback)
15 14 13 12 11
10 9 8 7 6 5 4 3 2 1

ISBN 978 1 406 22575 4 (paperback)
16 15 14 13 12
10 9 8 7 6 5 4 3 2 1

British Library Cataloguing in Publication Data
Ganeri, Anita, 1961-
 Canyon hunters. -- (Landform adventurers)
 1. Canyons--Juvenile literature.
 I. Title II. Series
 551.4'42-dc22

Acknowledgements
We would like to thank the following for permission to reproduce photographs: Alamy pp. 8 (© Manfred Gottschalk), 15 (© Design Pics Inc.), 29 (© Aurora Photos); Corbis pp. 11 (© Whit Richardson/Aurora Photos), 21 (© Craig Lovell), 25 (© Gerald & Buff Corsi/Visuals Unlimited), 26 (© STRINGER/EGYPT/Reuters); Getty Images pp. 7 (Gordon Wiltsie/National Geographic), 18 (Tom Walker/Stone), 20 (Gordon Wiltsie/National Geographic), 24 (Emory Kristof/National Geographic), 27 (Dave Hamman/Gallo Images); Photolibrary pp. 4 (Enrique Aguirre), 10 (Thomas J Brownold), 16 (EPA), 17 (John Cancalosi), 19 (Gilles Barbier); Science Photo Library p. 28 (Pascal Goetgheluck); Shutterstock pp. 5 (© zschnepf), 6 (© Mittep), 12 (© Xavier Marchant), 13 (© oksana.perkins), 14 (© Kushch Dmitry), 22 (© Bryan Brazil), 23 (© Danny Ortega). Cover photograph of a man hiking through a slot canyon near Moab, Utah reproduced with permission of Photolibrary (Bill Stevenson).

Every effort has been made to contact copyright holders of material reproduced in this book. Any omissions will be rectified in subsequent printings if notice is given to the publisher.

Disclaimer
All the Internet addresses (URLs) given in this book were valid at the time of going to press. However, due to the dynamic nature of the Internet, some addresses may have changed, or sites may have changed or ceased to exist since publication. While the author and publisher regret any inconvenience this may cause readers, no responsibility for any such changes can be accepted by either the author or the publisher.

Some words are shown in bold, **like this**. You can find out what they mean by looking in the glossary.

Contents

Cool canyons 4
Carving canyons .6
Canyons of the world 8
Canyon explorers 10
Canyons on land 12
Rock record 14
Fossil finds 16
Canyon wildlife 18
Roving rivers 20
Canyon homes 22
Underwater canyons 24
Desert canyons 26
Becoming a canyon hunter 28
Glossary 30
Find out more 31
Index 32

Cool canyons

Canyons are long, deep gashes in the Earth's surface. Canyons are also called gorges, ravines, and chasms.

Canyons are brilliant places to explore. Are you ready to go canyon hunting?

CANYON FACT
Some canyons are many kilometres across. Others are just wide enough to squeeze through.

Carving canyons

Colossal canyons are carved out of the rocks by rivers. As the water flows, it wears away the rocks on either side. Over millions of years, the canyon gets deeper and wider. This wearing away is called **erosion**.

Gorge du Verdon Canyon, France

CANYON FACT

The Yarlung Zangbo Canyon in China is more than six kilometres deep! That's deeper than 18 Eiffel Towers, standing on top of each other.

Canyons of the world

You can explore canyons in many different parts of the world. They are often found in dry places where it is easier for rivers to wear away the rocks.

The huge Copper Canyon in Mexico is actually a group of six canyons.

This map shows some of the most famous canyons on Earth.

Tara River Canyon, Montenegro

Yarlung Zangbo Canyon, China

Kings Canyon, Australia

Fish River Canyon, Namibia

Grand Canyon, USA

Copper Canyon, Mexico

Canyon explorers

Many different scientists study canyons:

- **Geologists** study canyon rocks.
- **Palaeontologists** study **fossils**.
- **Biologists** study wildlife.
- **Archaeologists** study things from the past.

CANYON FACT
Some people like to go canyoneering. That means climbing canyons for fun!

Hydrologists are scientists who study canyon rivers.

Canyons on land

Some spectacular canyons are found on land. The Grand Canyon, in the United States, is almost 450 kilometres long and two kilometres deep. That is as deep as four Empire State Buildings standing on top of each other.

Grand Canyon, Arizona, USA

mule

Scientists reach the canyon by plane, helicopter, and kayak. They also hike, climb, or ride down on mules.

Rock record

As a river flows through a canyon, it shows up different layers in the rocks. **Geologists** study the rocks to find out more about the story of Earth. The oldest rocks are at the bottom. The youngest rocks are at the top.

layers

CANYON FACT

The rocks at the bottom of the Grand Canyon are almost two billion years old.

Fossil finds

The rocks in a canyon are so old that there are often **fossils** hidden inside. **Palaeontologists** study these fossils.

This ancient whale is 40 million years old!

CANYON FACT
There are no dinosaur fossils in the Grand Canyon. The rocks are too old!

Trilobites were alive long before dinosaurs existed.

In the Grand Canyon, people have found fossils of sea creatures such as trilobites. Ancient footprints of reptiles, scorpions, and centipedes have been found there too!

Canyon wildlife

Many amazing animals live in canyons. In the Grand Canyon, **biologists** fit **satellite radio collars** to mountain lions. They use these to track the lions and learn more about them.

In the Colca Canyon in Peru, biologists ride into the canyon on horseback to study birds called Andean condors.

CANYON FACT

Andean condors have a wingspan of more than three metres. Imagine 15 footballs in a row – that's how big their wings are!

Roving rivers

Some rivers flow through canyons. **Hydrologists** are scientists who study river wildlife, and look at how rivers flow and flood.

Yarlung Zangbo Canyon, China

The river in the Yarlung Zangbo Canyon can be very dangerous to travel on.

CANYON FACT

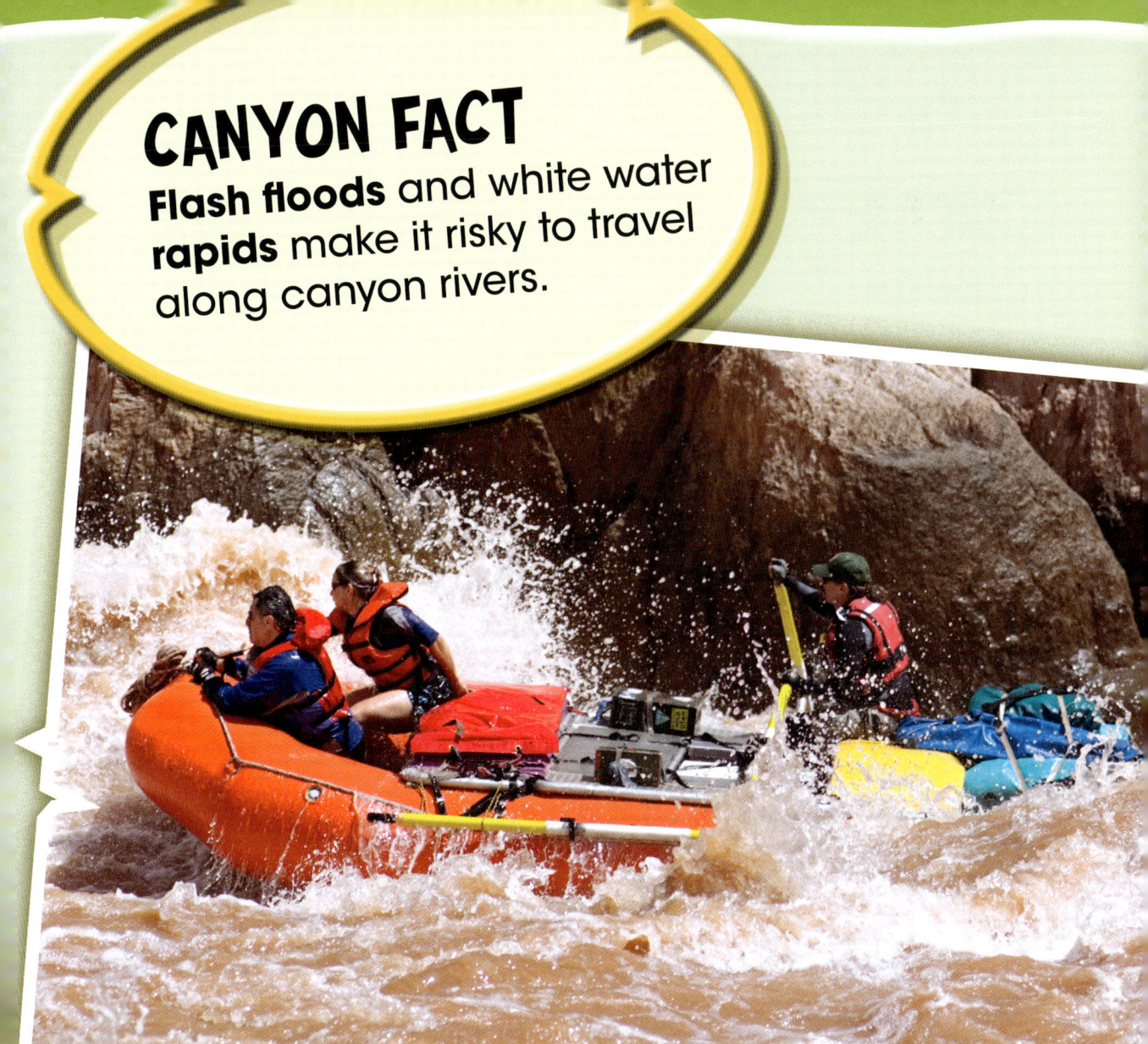

Flash floods and white water **rapids** make it risky to travel along canyon rivers.

Hydrologists use rafts and kayaks to travel along the rivers. They sometimes camp on the river banks.

Canyon homes

Some canyons were homes to ancient people. You can still see the ruins of their buildings in the canyon walls. **Archaeologists** study these ruins and look for clues about how people lived in the past.

Cliff Palace, Colorado, USA

Carvings at the Canyon De Chelly, Arizona, USA

CANYON FACT
Drawings and carvings from ancient people have been found on canyon walls.

Underwater canyons

Canyons are also found under the sea. To study them, scientists use mini submarines, called **submersibles**. Cameras on board boats take videos of what they see.

submersible

CANYON FACT
Strange and mysterious creatures can be found in deep, underwater canyons. Some are blind. Others have no colour!

sea cucumber

Desert canyons

Desert canyons are called **wadis**. Wadis are usually dry, but they fill up after heavy rain. To study them, scientists travel in specially designed cars. They have to be careful. A **flash flood** could suddenly sweep down a wadi and wash them away.

CANYON FACT
In 2005 **biologists** discovered tiny fish living in wadis in the Middle East.

Becoming a canyon hunter

If you want to become a canyon hunter, you need to be good at science. You may also need to study a subject such as **geology** at university.

CANYON FACT
Some canyons are in places where very few people go. So there are plenty left for you to explore!

Being a canyon hunter is an exciting career. Sometimes, you might be based in a laboratory. You may also get to travel to canyons all over the world!

Glossary

archaeologist scientist who studies things from the past

biologist scientist who studies living things

erosion how rocks are worn away by wind and water

flash floods floods that happen very quickly after heavy rain

fossils remains of ancient plants and animals that have turned to stone

geologist scientist who studies the Earth

geology study of rocks, minerals, and soil

hydrologist scientist who studies water

palaeontologist [say "pale-e-on-tol-o-gist"] scientist who studies fossils

rapids fast-moving water in a river

satellite radio collar collar that uses satellites to track an animal's movements

submersible vehicle like a mini submarine, used for exploring the deep sea

wadis canyons in the desert that are usually dry

Find out more

Books

100 Things You Should Know about Extreme Earth, Belinda Gallagher (Miles Kelly, 2009)

Horrible Geography: Raging Rivers, Anita Ganeri (Scholastic Children's Books, 2008)

Natural Wonders: Canyons, Alyse Sweeney (Capstone, 2010)

Websites

www.canyonsworldwide.com
This site has lots of facts and pictures of amazing canyons around the world.

www.rockwatch.org.uk/
Rockwatch is a club for young geologists. It is linked to the Geologists Association.

www.strange-facts.info/interesting-grand-canyon-facts
Find out some interesting facts about the Grand Canyon on this website.

Find out
Where can you find the Rainbow Plateau?

Index

ancient peoples 22–23
archaeologists 10, 22
Australia 9

becoming a canyon hunter 28–29
biologists 10, 18, 19, 27

Canyon De Chelly 23
canyoneering 11
chasms 4
China 7, 9, 20
Cliff Palace 22
Colca Canyon 19, 23
condors 19
Copper Canyon 8, 9

desert canyons 26–27

erosion 6, 8

Fish River Canyon 9
flash floods 21, 26
formation of canyons 6
fossils 10, 16–17
France 6

geologists 10, 14
Gorge du Verdon 6
gorges 4
Grand Canyon 9, 12–13, 15, 16, 17, 18

homes 22–23
hydrologists 11, 20, 21

Incas 23

Kings Canyon 9

Mexico 8, 9
Montenegro 9
mountain lions 18

Namibia 9

palaeontologists 10, 16
Peru 19, 23

rapids 21
ravines 4
rivers 6, 8, 11, 14, 20–21
rocks 6, 8, 10, 14–15, 16

submersibles 24

Tara River Canyon 9
trilobites 17

underwater canyons 24–25
USA 9, 12–13, 15, 16, 17, 18, 22, 23

wadis 26–27
wildlife 10, 18–19, 20, 25, 27

Yarlung Zangbo Canyon 7, 9, 20